The Decade of the 2000s

Terrorism and War of the 2000s

Other titles in *The Decade of the 2000s* series:

The Decade of the 2000s

Terrorism and War of the 2000s

By Patricia D. Netzley

ReferencePoint
Press®

San Diego, CA

© 2014 ReferencePoint Press, Inc.
Printed in the United States

For more information, contact:
ReferencePoint Press, Inc.
PO Box 27779
San Diego, CA 92198
www.ReferencePointPress.com

LIBRARY OF CONGRESS CATALOGING-IN-PUBLICATION DATA

Netzley, Patricia D.
  Terrorism and war of the 2000s / by Patricia D. Netzley.
     pages cm -- (The decade of the 2000s series)
  Includes bibliographical references and index.
  ISBN-13: 978-1-60152-530-7 (hardback)
  ISBN-10: 1-60152-530-3 (hardback)
  1. Terrorism--History--21st century. 2. War--History--21st century. I. Title.
  HV6431.N4819 2014
  363.325--dc23
                                                                            2012049462

Contents

Important Events of the **2000s**

2002
- Euro enters circulation
- Terrorists attack Bali tourist district in Indonesia
- Dwarf planet Quaoar is discovered
- *American Idol* debuts on Fox network
- Xbox Live revolutionizes online gaming

2004
- Hundreds of thousands die in Indian Ocean tsunami
- *Spirit* and *Opportunity* rovers explore surface of Mars
- Facebook is launched
- Hundreds die when Chechen separatists take over a school in Russia
- Palestinian leader Yasser Arafat dies
- Green Belt Movement founder Wangari Maathai of Kenya wins Nobel Peace Prize

2000
- Dire warnings of Y2K Millennium Bug fizzle
- Dot-com bubble bursts
- Israel withdraws all forces from Lebanon
- Dashboard GPS devices become widely available
- Tiger Woods becomes youngest golfer to win Grand Slam
- USS *Cole* is attacked in Yemen

2000 2001 2002 2003 2004

2001
- Terrorist attack on United States kills three thousand people
- Apple launches iPod
- World's first space tourist reaches International Space Station
- Film version of first Harry Potter book is released
- Wikipedia is launched
- United States invades Afghanistan
- Netherlands legalizes same-sex marriage

2003
- United States invades Iraq
- Space shuttle *Columbia* disintegrates on reentry
- Human genome project is completed
- Record heat wave kills tens of thousands in Europe
- China launches its first manned space mission
- WHO issues rare global health alert on SARS

2005
- YouTube is launched
- Burst levees flood New Orleans during Hurricane Katrina
- Kyoto Protocol on climate change goes into effect
- National Academies releases human embryonic stem cell research guidelines
- Earthquake devastates Kashmir
- Lance Armstrong wins seventh consecutive Tour de France (later stripped of all titles)

2008
- United States elects Barack Obama, first African American president
- Oil prices hit record high of $147 per barrel
- US Olympic swimmer Michael Phelps wins record eight gold medals
- Islamic militants attack financial district in Mumbai, India
- Universal Declaration of Human Rights marks sixtieth anniversary

2005   2006   2007   2008   2009

2006
- Pluto is demoted to dwarf planet status
- North Korea conducts its first nuclear test
- Saddam Hussein is executed in Iraq
- West African black rhino is declared extinct
- Twitter is launched
- Global warming documentary, *An Inconvenient Truth*, is released

2009
- WHO declares swine flu outbreak an international pandemic
- Mouse genome is fully sequenced
- Michael Jackson dies at his home in California
- World's tallest man-made structure is completed in Dubai
- Large Hadron Collider becomes world's highest-energy particle accelerator
- Widespread match-fixing scandal rocks European soccer

2007
- Mitchell report details rampant PED use in baseball
- Apple debuts iPhone
- Dozens killed and wounded in mass shooting at Virginia Tech
- Arctic sea ice hits record low
- Google Street View is launched
- Prime Minister Benazir Bhutto of Pakistan is assassinated
- Amazon releases its Kindle
- Great Recession, worldwide economic crisis, begins

A Climate of Fear

Less than two years into the twenty-first century, more than three thousand people died in a single, coordinated terrorist attack that stunned the world. This attack heralded a decade during which terrorism, wars, and civil strife brought pain, suffering, and death to countless people in nations both wealthy and poor. The global reach of terrorism during the first decade of the 2000s produced a climate of fear even in places where such attacks were rare.

In fact, fear of terrorist attacks was so prevalent during the decade that it made one American politician, Senator John McCain, exhort in his 2004 book *Why Courage Matters*:

> Calculate the odds of being harmed by a terrorist! It's still about as likely as being swept out to sea by a tidal wave. Suck it up, for crying out loud. You're almost certainly going to be okay. And in the unlikely event you're not, do you really want to spend your last days cowering behind plastic sheets and duct tape [sealing your windows and doors in hopes of keeping out biological or chemical weapons]? That's not a life worth living, is it?[1]

Fanatics

Warranted or not, fear spread throughout the decade—helped in large part by the rise of violent fanaticism. Fanatics are people motivated by extreme, unreasoning devotion to a cause, and during the 2000s more and more fanatics were drawn to terrorist causes throughout the world. Among these fanatics were members of al Qaeda, a loosely organized group that interpreted the teachings of their Muslim faith as being a directive to kill those who did not follow these teachings, particularly Americans. This was the group responsible for the first major coordinated terrorist attack of the 2000s.

The attack involved nineteen al Qaeda members, fifteen of them from Saudi Arabia, the native country of the group's leader, Osama bin Laden. The men's goal was to hijack several airliners and use them as weapons by flying them into high-profile buildings that symbolized American life and values: the twin towers of the World Trade Center in New York City (representing the US economy), the Pentagon building (the US military), and the White House (the US government). In preparation for the attack, some of the plotters attended flight schools in the United States to learn how to pilot American passenger jets, and others tested whether they could smuggle knives on board various flights without interference.

Once ready, the plotters bought tickets on four flights scheduled for September 11, 2001: American Airlines Flight 11 leaving Boston, Massachusetts, at 8:00 a.m.; American Airlines Flight 175 leaving Boston at 8:15 a.m.; United Airlines Flight 77 leaving an airport near Washington, DC, at 8:20 a.m.; and United Airlines Flight 93 leaving Newark, New Jersey, at 8:45 a.m. Their original plan called for five men to board each plane, but after one member of their group, Zacharias Moussaoui, was jailed by the FBI for overstaying the visa that allowed him to visit the United States, the attackers decided that Flight 93 would carry only four of them.

All of the tickets were for first-class seats because this would put the attackers nearest to each plane's cockpit. In addition, all of the flights were traveling nonstop to California, so that each plane was carrying a large amount of fuel. Fuel can explode on impact, and if this happens, the more fuel there is the bigger the blast. The attackers were hoping not just to damage their targets in a crash but also to blow them up.

Hitting the Twin Towers

The men waited to begin their attack until the planes were airborne, timing their actions so that all buildings would be hit at roughly the same time. The five on Flight 11 and the five on Flight 175 were apparently successful in carrying out the plan as it was envisioned, attacking passengers and flight attendants with box cutters and knives they had smuggled on board, forcing their way into the cockpit, killing or severely wounding the flight crew, and taking control of the plane. Flight 11 was then flown toward the north Trade Center tower while Flight 175 headed for the south tower. The planes hit their respective targets at 8:48 and 9:06 a.m.

An Australian tourist, identifying herself only as Penny, later told reporters what she had seen from her hotel room across the street from the twin towers: "I was standing at the window taking photos of the view when I heard the sound of the plane approaching. It seemed normal at first until in a few split seconds it turned into a roar, followed by a massive explosion. I'm sure as I can be that whoever was flying that jet put it in full throttle just before it hit, as the screech sounded just like when a plane is taking off."[2]

Penny then saw people in the tower breaking windows and jumping to their deaths. Shortly thereafter, she saw the second plane hit. "The explosion was a lot bigger and closer and our building shook. I suddenly realised something was very wrong."[3] Afraid that her own building would

Smoke billows from one of the World Trade Center's twin towers moments before a second hijacked plane plunges into the adjacent tower. The 2001 terrorist attack on the United States, which resulted in more than three thousand deaths, heralded a decade of violence and fear.

be hit next, she raced from her hotel and ran away from the chaos as fast as she could. Glass and debris were raining down, bodies continued to fall. Meanwhile, people inside the towers, some of them horribly injured, were trying to escape down smoke-filled stairwells. One secretary later told a reporter, "There were so many running down the stairs; running over each other and screaming and pushing and trying to get out. And that was before the tower came down."[4]

First the south tower collapsed, and then, about thirty minutes later, the north tower fell. The following day a description of the first collapse appeared in the British newspaper the *Guardian*, which had correspondents on the scene. They wrote: "As the crowds stood paralysed, one of the towers then did the unthinkable: it suddenly disappeared into a cloud of its own making, and, in slow motion, collapsed to the ground with a deadly, horrible thud—punctured by screams on the streets. . . . People sprinted north, chased by the grey-black smoke and rubble, mouths dry with terror and dust."[5]

Not as Planned

Meanwhile, the attackers on the other two planes had been attempting to hit their targets at around the same time as their associates. The five on Flight 77 took control of their plane over New York, piloted it to nearby Arlington, Virginia, and flew it into the Pentagon. They did not realize that most of the building section they aimed for had been closed for renovations, which meant the strike killed fewer people than they had hoped.

The four attackers on Flight 93 took control of their plane while it was over Ohio and flew it back toward Washington, DC. Before the terrorists could reach their target, passengers on the plane learned about the events at the World Trade Center from cell phone conversations with loved ones at home, who were watching the crisis unfold on television. Realizing they were going to die in a similar attack, some of the passengers decided to try to gain control of the plane. During the ensuing battle, Flight 93 crashed to the ground in a western Pennsylvania field.

All 40 people on the plane were killed, but no one on the ground was hurt. In the strike on the Pentagon, all 59 people aboard the plane and 184 in the building died. Approximately 3,000 in the World Trade Center were killed along with 147 people on the two planes. In addition, several hundred rescue workers died valiantly trying to save people from the buildings.

A World Ravaged by Violence

The scenes of terror, panic, and ruin traveled quickly around the world. Reporters dubbed the attack *9/11* and speculated on the possibility that similar attacks were imminent both in America and abroad. FBI officials warned that as many as five thousand more al Qaeda operatives were suspected of hiding in American cities waiting to strike. Although this warning later proved to be without foundation, the horrifyingly vivid images and other official statements heightened fear and anxiety worldwide but especially in the United States. As anthropologist Scott Atran said of the 9/11 terrorists in 2011, "Perhaps never in the history of human conflict have so few people with so few capabilities frightened so many."[6]

But the United States was far from the only country to experience the ravages of violence, terrorism, and war in the 2000s. In the tourist district of Bali in Indonesia, terrorists bombed popular cafés. In Darfur, located in the North African country of Sudan, thousands of people were brutally tortured and killed by members of a government-backed militia. In Spain, members of an ethnic group fighting for an independent state committed acts of terrorism in hopes of furthering their cause. In Haiti, rebel attacks led to the ouster of an elected president. These events and many others added to the growing sense during the decade that the world was becoming an increasingly dangerous and violent place.

Chapter ONE

The War on Terror

Led by the United States and its close ally the United Kingdom, the War on Terror was an international military campaign launched in 2001 as a direct response to the 9/11 attacks on American soil. Its original goal was to eliminate all Islamic extremists who belonged to al Qaeda, the group responsible for the attacks, and anyone who had aided al Qaeda. "We'll have to deal with the [terrorism] networks," said Secretary of Defense Donald Rumsfeld during a press briefing just seven days after 9/11. "One of the ways to do that is to drain the swamp they live in. And that means dealing not only with the terrorists, but those who harbor terrorists."[7]

The United States called on other nations to come to its aid, and ultimately more than seventy countries lent their support to the campaign, turning it into a global effort. As time passed, the objectives of the War on Terror expanded beyond capturing Osama bin Laden and destroying al Qaeda. The War on Terror sought to destroy terrorists and terrorist organizations, stop those who provided terrorists with support or sanctuary, foster democratic ideals and institutions, and promote policies that protect people from terrorist attacks. The War on Terror became not just a military campaign but also a political, legal, and ideological battle against terrorists, terrorist organizations, and terrorism as a whole.

The Patriot Act

In the United States, the document that made possible the prosecution of the War on Terror was the Patriot Act—signed into law by President George W. Bush on October 26, 2001. Its formal name, the USA Patriot Act, stood for Uniting and Strengthening America by Providing Appropriate Tools Required to Intercept and Obstruct Terrorism Act.

The Patriot Act broadened the power of law enforcement agencies in regard to gathering information, detaining foreigners for questioning, interfering with financial transactions, and engaging in other activities designed to combat terrorism both inside and outside the United States.

From the beginning, the Patriot Act was controversial. Some people lauded it for making it easier for the government to deter terrorism and capture terrorists. Others argued that it gave the government too much power to violate civil liberties. For example, the law gave intelligence and military agencies greater power to spy on American citizens if those citizens were suspected of aiding terrorists or otherwise supporting terrorism. It also made it easier for authorities to gather details about a person's Internet use.

Many people called for parts or all of the act to be struck down. For example, US congressman Ron Paul said,

> I think the Patriot Act is unpatriotic because it undermines our liberty. I'm concerned, as everybody is, about the terrorist attack. . . . But why I really fear it is we have drifted into a condition that we were warned against because our early founders were very clear. They said, don't be willing to sacrifice liberty for security. Today it seems too easy that our government and our congresses are so willing to give up our liberties for our security.[8]

Despite views such as those expressed by Paul, Congress reauthorized the act three times during the 2000s.

An Ultimatum to the Taliban

Meanwhile, the United States and its allies in the War on Terror were conducting military strikes on terrorists and their supporters abroad. The war's first target was Afghanistan, a landlocked country of about 30 million in southern Asia. US experts believed that while the al Qaeda organization recruited members throughout the world, many were actually trained in Afghanistan. This belief was based in large part on the fact that the group was allied with the Taliban regime then in control of the Afghan government.

thousand US Marines. In the meantime, NATO increased its forces to thirty-two thousand. Nonetheless, in October 2009, 58 US troops were killed in Afghanistan, and on December 1, 2009, Obama sent thirty thousand more troops into the country, leaving the war unresolved at the end of the decade.

PERSPECTIVES

The War on Terror Saved Few Lives

Americans opposed to the War on Terror had many reasons for believing it was the wrong response to 9/11. Some felt it was wrong to counter violence with violence. Others believed that Iraq and Afghanistan were the wrong targets to choose in order to strike back at al Qaeda.

Still others focused on claims that the war had saved many American lives. In exploring this belief, Erica Frank, a physician and associate professor with the Department of Family and Preventive Medicine at Emory University's School of Medicine in Atlanta, Georgia, determined that far more people die in the United States from preventable diseases than from terrorism. On the same day that thirty-four hundred people died because of the plane crashes on 9/11, another fifty-two hundred Americans died from common diseases, she said. Yet in September 2002, the state of New York was given only $1.3 million in federal funds to fight heart disease—the number-one cause of death among New Yorkers. In contrast, the state received $34 million to combat and respond to bioterrorism threats. Frank explained:

> Predictable tragedies happen every day. We know strategies to reduce deaths from tobacco, alcohol, poor diet, unintentional injuries, and other predictable causes. And we know that millions of people will die unless we protect the population against these routine causes of death. . . . Since the point of investing in counterterror is to protect American lives, the question [is:] is a dollar better spent in Iraq or is it better spent here?"

Quoted in Maggie Fox, "'War on Terror' Saves Few Lives: Expert," Common Dreams, September 9, 2005. www.common dreams.org.

The Iraq War

With the assault and rebuilding effort in Afghanistan barely under way, the United States expanded its War on Terror to a second front: the Middle Eastern country of Iraq. In 2002 US president Bush and British prime minister Tony Blair accused the government of Iraq, then under dictator Saddam Hussein, of supporting terrorist groups, including al Qaeda. They also accused the country of having and making weapons of mass destruction (WMDs)—nuclear, biological, and chemical weapons—that threatened international peace.

As a result of these complaints, the United Nations (UN) Security Council passed a resolution on November 8, 2002, calling on Iraq to allow inspectors into the country to confirm that this was not the case. It was not the first time such a demand had been made. During the prior decade, as a result of other conflicts, the UN had banned Iraq from possessing WMDs. After Iraq refused to allow inspections to verify that it was not violating the ban, US and British forces bombed the sites where the weapons were believed to be manufactured and/or stored. But this time, after much negotiation, Iraq did allow inspections, and no WMDs were found.

Bush and Blair rejected this result, saying Saddam had tricked the inspectors. They demanded the UN authorize another attack on Iraq. Other world leaders, including those in France, Germany, and Russia, disagreed that an attack was necessary, and the UN hesitated to act. But Bush decided to take action anyway. On March 17, 2003, he told Saddam to leave Iraq within forty-eight days or there would be war. When Saddam refused, Bush ordered an attack on Iraq.

On March 20, air raid sirens went off in Iraq's capital city, Baghdad, as US warships in the Red Sea and the Persian Gulf began firing satellite-guided Tomahawk cruise missiles at various military and government targets. Meanwhile, F117 stealth fighters dropped 2,000-pound (907 kg) bombs on the country, and nearly three hundred thousand US and UK troops massed in the Persian Gulf region to ready themselves for a ground attack. A few days later this force invaded Iraq from Kuwait, joined by about two thousand soldiers from Australia and nearly two hundred from Poland. Soon dozens of countries committed troops as well—forty-nine countries in all—and on April 9 Baghdad fell to the invaders. The rest of Iraq was taken over by April 14, and although Saddam had escaped capture, on May 1, 2003, Bush declared that major combat operations in Iraq had ended.

The Aftermath of the War

Some Iraqis celebrated the ousting of Saddam, others vowed revenge on the invaders, and still others had mixed feelings. Baghdad fruit vendor Osama Yessin, for example, told reporter Robert Collier on the day Baghdad fell, "This is good. The Americans are welcome," but minutes later he said, "But we will fight the Americans, and they will all die."[12] In his article, Collier speculated that this might be a case of someone unfamiliar with freedom clinging to "old survival instincts and old habits"[13] acquired under a dictator whose whims made it unsafe to take sides.

As the Iraqis dealt with their new situation, the United States continued to search both for Saddam and for WMDs. At one point Bush announced that Iraq's WMDs were in hand. A White House spokesman later admitted that this was not the case, and Bush himself subsequently confirmed he had been mistaken. To date, there is still no evidence that Iraq actually had WMDs.

The United States had more success with its hunt for Saddam. On December 13, 2003, an informant's tip led US troops to a farm in Tikrit, a town near the dictator's birthplace. There they found a hole that someone had attempted to conceal with a scrap of carpet, a piece of plastic, some bricks, and some dirt. The leader of the search, Colonel James Hickey, ordered that a hand grenade be thrown into the hole, but before this could happen, a person emerged. "Two hands appeared," Hickey later said. "The individual [inside the hole] clearly wanted to surrender."[14]

Although confused and disoriented when pulled from the hole, the man identified himself as Saddam and said he wanted to negotiate for his release. Instead, he was imprisoned in Iraq. Two other people at the farm believed to have been helping Saddam were also imprisoned.

When US soldiers searched the hideaway, they discovered that it was actually a 6-foot by 8-foot (1.8 m by 2.4 m) underground chamber with an air vent and fan. Near the hole was a mud hut consisting of two rooms, a bedroom, and a kitchen with running water; officials suspected Saddam used the hut during his time in hiding. The search also turned up $750,000 in cash, two AK-47 assault rifles, and a document-filled briefcase.

Attempts to Rebuild Iraq

During the hunt for Saddam, coalition forces had begun efforts to help Iraqis rebuild their country and establish a new government. This was not an easy task. Immediately after the regime collapsed, widespread looting began, mostly targeting government offices and other public buildings. Violence between Iraq's two major Muslim populations, the Shiites and Sunnis, and between these Iraqi Arabs and the country's Kurdish population, also increased. Coalition forces were also targeted in attacks.

By November 2004, deaths of US troops had reached one thousand, and by early 2007 this number had exceeded three thousand. Bush responded by temporarily increasing the number of US troops by more than twenty thousand, an event known as the troop surge. Meanwhile, sectarian violence among Muslims continued. Although it is hard to tell how many Iraqis died as a result of this violence, most experts believe that the number of war-related Iraqi deaths in the country between 2003 and 2009 was at least one hundred thousand. Meanwhile, the number of countries participating in the coalition dropped from thirty-seven in 2004 to twenty-six in 2008, the year that the United States agreed to start withdrawing from Iraq. But there was no chance of Saddam regaining control of the country. In late 2006 he had been sentenced to death and had been hanged for his attempts over a decade earlier to exterminate the country's Kurdish and Shiite populations.

Continuing Efforts

Even as the United States and its allies were fighting terrorists in Iraq and Afghanistan, they were working to combat terrorism elsewhere in the world. To this end, on February 14, 2003, President Bush issued a document called the National Strategy for Combating Terrorism. In that document he stated that the United States would focus

> on taking the fight to the terrorists themselves. We are using all elements of our national power and international influence to attack terror networks; reduce their ability to communicate and coordinate their plans; isolate them from potential allies and

from each other; and identify and disrupt their plots before they attack. Our country works closely with every nation committed to this fight, and we will continue to help our allies and friends improve their ability to fight terror.[15]

One such friend was Pakistan, although the friendship was a tenuous one. For much of the 2000s, some American officials suspected that terrorist organizations had, with Pakistan's knowledge, established bases in remote parts of the country. Pakistani leaders rejected this view, noting that they had allowed the United States to use their air bases as part of the War on Terror and that this aid often led terrorists to retaliate against Pakistan.

In fact, terrorist attacks on Pakistan became so problematic that in 2004 the country launched a series of attacks against Taliban and al Qaeda insurgents in Waziristan, a region on the country's northwest border with Afghanistan. This conflict, the Waziristan War, continued throughout the decade. Toward the end of the decade, the US military began using remote-controlled aircraft, known as drones, as well as commandos on the ground to attack terrorist havens in remote parts of Pakistan.

The Costs of War

US antiterrorism efforts in Pakistan, Iraq, and Afghanistan came with costs in both money and lives. In June 2011, researchers with Brown University's Watson Institute for International Studies announced the results of an analysis of just what those costs were. The institute's Costs of War project had determined that over the previous ten years, warfare in the three countries had taken at least 225,000 lives. This included more than 31,000 members of coalition forces and military contractors and at least 137,000 civilians. The wars also turned more than 7.8 million citizens of Iraq, Afghanistan, and Pakistan into refugees.

The economic cost of the War on Terror was also huge. According to the Brown study, America had spent an estimated $4 trillion, an amount that included interest fees for loans used to finance the war and between $600 billion to $950 billion in costs related to the current and future care of disabled war veterans. In addition, according to project codirector Neta Crawford,

> There are many costs and consequences of war that cannot be quantified, and the consequences of wars don't end when the fighting stops. . . . [Our project] has made [only] a start at counting and estimating the costs in blood, treasure, and lost opportunities that are both immediately visible and those which are less visible and likely to grow even when the fighting winds down.[16]

There is also a cost to housing prisoners from the wars. For example, each of the roughly 170 suspected terrorists held at the Guantánamo Bay naval base in Cuba costs the United States $800,000 a year. According to *Miami Herald* reporter Carol Rosenberg, "The Pentagon detention center that started out in January 2002 as a collection of crude open-air cells guarded by Marines in a muddy tent city is today arguably the most expensive prison on earth."[17] Experts say that the expense is largely due to the fact that all supplies must be flown in to the base or brought there by barge. Consequently, officials had planned to shut the facility down in 2009, and no new prisoners were sent there after March 2008, but it continued to operate in 2013.

Unintended Consequences

Some experts say that the fighting in Afghanistan, Iraq, and Pakistan had another cost: a strengthening of support systems for terrorists elsewhere. With so many resources being devoted to these three countries, there was little left to combat terrorism elsewhere. But it was also due to the belief among many Muslims that the United States wanted to take over these countries because Westerners are anti-Muslim, an idea that drew many new recruits to terrorist groups.

The events in Afghanistan and Iraq also led to the strengthening of neighboring Iran, which had long considered the United States its enemy. Without Afghanistan's Taliban and Iraq's Saddam to oppose it, Iran's influence in the region grew, and so did support for its Islamic extremism. At the same time, Iran began working with the Taliban to oppose US forces. In reporting on this situation for the television network CNN, Iranian American religious scholar Reza Aslan explained, "The

Military police keep a watchful eye on detainees (in orange jumpsuits) awaiting processing at the US Navy's Guantánamo Bay detention center in Cuba in 2002. Despite various efforts to close the costly facility, it continued to operate in 2013.

last thing Iran wants to see is a permanent American presence in its back-yard. This would be disastrous for Iran's national security, as far as they're concerned. So they're willing to do whatever it takes, including working with al Qaeda, working with certain Taliban forces."[18] As a result, by the end of the 2000s some experts were questioning the benefits of the War on Terror, pondering whether it had been worth the cost in lives, money, and political stability.

Chapter TWO

Hostage Taking

During the 2000s, at least two thousand people were taken hostage by terrorists or others fighting for a political cause. According to Minwoo Yun, an expert in such crimes, this was a significant increase from previous decades. He says, "Since the mid 1990s, hostage taking and kidnapping have dramatically increased as a preferred tactic of political terrorists. . . . Hostage taking and kidnapping has become one of the most valued weapons in the modern terrorist arsenal."[19] Hostages might be used as bargaining chips to gain political concessions, or they might be killed in order to make a political statement. Yun reports that by 2005, terrorists were also relying on hostage taking as a way to earn money, through ransoms, to support their activities.

This was particularly true in Afghanistan and Iraq. Between 2004 and 2010, Islamic extremists took thousands of their countrymen hostage specifically to raise money for their terrorist activities. They also kidnapped hundreds of foreigners, many of them contractors working on projects that aided the war effort. In such cases the kidnappers were sometimes motivated by the hope that their victims' loved ones, employers, or governments would pay for their release. Often, however, the kidnappers demanded political concessions in exchange for the hostages' release and killed the hostages if these demands were not met. Occasionally they killed a hostage as a political statement without making any demands, or at least without the public becoming aware that any demands had been made.

Nick Berg

Demanding political concessions in exchange for a hostage was a factor in one of the most notorious kidnappings of the decade, that of twenty-six-year-old Nick Berg. Berg, a US citizen, went to Iraq in 2004 because he had heard that he could make $20,000 a month there as a communications-tower repairman. The job paid well for two reasons. First, it required the repairman to climb hundreds of feet into the air, sometimes in 120°F (49°C) heat. Second, Iraq was a dangerous place, especially for Westerners following Saddam's ouster.

But Berg did not worry about the dangers of the region. In fact, he was careless about his safety. *Time* magazine later reported, "In a country where foreign businessmen are reluctant to travel even in armor-clad SUVs with security guards, Nick Berg crisscrossed Iraq by hailing cabs and hopping onto buses. Usually clad in a baseball cap and jeans, he made no effort to blend in with the locals as he lugged around sophisticated electronic equipment in search of work."[20]

Berg, who was Jewish, had traveled to Iraq by way of Israel, which meant he had an Israeli stamp in his passport. This caused him trouble in Iraq, where anti-Israel (and anti-Jewish) sentiments were strong; some people believe it might have been the reason he was targeted for kidnapping. In any case, in March 2004, while passing through a checkpoint in the Iraqi city of Mosul, Berg aroused the suspicions of police. They took him to a Baghdad prison for questioning. Thirteen days later, on April 6, Berg was released, but four days after that he disappeared after checking out of a Baghdad hotel.

A month later US soldiers found Berg's headless body on a Baghdad overpass. Three days after that, on May 11, someone posted a video on the Internet entitled "Abu Musa'b al-Zarqawi Slaughters an American." This graphic five-minute video showed Berg, in an orange jumpsuit, surrounded by five men in ski masks. Speaking to the camera, Berg identified himself, recited the names of family members, and said he was from Pennsylvania. Then one of the men read aloud a lengthy statement complaining about the treatment of Muslim prisoners in the US Army–run Abu-Ghraib prison in Iraq. After this, two of the men held Berg down as he was decapitated with a knife while the men cheered and Berg screamed.

The man who had read the statement was later confirmed by voice analysis to be Islamic terrorist Abu Musa'b al-Zarqawi. In his remarks, he stated the reason for Berg's killing:

Mothers and wives of the American soldiers, we say to you that we offered the American Administration the chance to exchange this prisoner for some of the prisoners in Abu-Ghraib, but they refused. We say to you, the dignity of the Muslim men and women in the prison of Abu-Ghraib and others will be redeemed by blood and souls. You will see nothing from us except corpse after corpse and casket after casket of those slaughtered in this fashion.[21]

Peter Moore

Other hostages in the Middle East died in a similarly horrific fashion, but some managed to escape this fate. This was the case with thirty-four-year-old British information technology consultant Peter Moore. On May 29, 2007, he was installing software at the Iraqi Finance Ministry in Baghdad when forty armed men wearing police uniforms burst in and seized him. The men also captured the four UK security guards employed by a Canadian firm to protect Moore.

Over the next two years the kidnappers—who identified themselves as an Islamic resistance group—threatened to kill the hostages one at a time unless the British government took certain actions. In a videotape made right after the hostages were taken, the kidnappers demanded that the government withdraw all of its troops from Iraq. In a later videotape they demanded that the government release specific Iraqi prisoners. As their demands kept changing, the British government kept stating publicly that it would not negotiate with terrorists.

Meanwhile, the families of the hostages made public pleas for their release. In response to one mother's plea, the kidnappers posted a message to her on the Internet: "We understand your feelings as a mother who misses her son and we ask you in return to feel for the Iraqi mothers who miss their children jailed in your government's prisons for no crime they committed."[22]

All the while, negotiators were working behind the scenes. Finally, in December 2009, Moore was released while dozens of Iraqis with ties to the kidnappers were quietly let out of prison. By this time the security guards were already dead. When their bodies were later provided to British authorities, experts determined they had been killed in 2008. In 2010 an Iraqi with connections to the kidnapping revealed that two of the guards had been gunned down in a street while running from a militant safe house where they were being held. Another was shot while trying to grab a gun that had been left on a table. The fourth was killed when his captors mistakenly thought their hideout was about to be stormed by rescuers.

Moore, held alone for most of his time in captivity, did not know the location of his hideout. Authorities thought that he had been taken over the border into Iran. Some also believed that Iran's Revolutionary Guard,

A video image broadcast in 2008 by an Arab news network shows British consultant Peter Moore, who was kidnapped in 2007 by militants disguised as Iraqi police officers. Moore was released in 2009 after dozens of Iraqis with ties to the kidnappers were released from prison.

Pay Ransoms for Hostages

Amidst refusals by the United States and the United Kingdom to pay ransom money for hostages, it became clear that paying ransom could save lives. For example, in 2009 terrorists kidnapped four people in Mali: two Swiss, a German, and a Briton. Sources in Switzerland and Germany paid $2.8 million for the release of their citizens, and the hostages were sent home unharmed. The United Kingdom, however, refused to pay ransom for their citizen, and the terrorists killed that person. Many hostages were also killed during the decade as a result of failed rescue missions launched by government officials who refused to meet the kidnappers' demands.

Therefore in countries where the policy was not to negotiate with terrorists, people—especially loved ones of the kidnap victims—often called for their officials to negotiate anyway. In discussing this issue, Brian Montopoli of CBS News said:

> Some argue that paying ransoms for hostages puts potential hostages . . . in greater danger in the future. And there are obvious concerns about paying a ransom that could effectively fund terrorist activities. But it's worth remembering that it's hard to think in general terms when attempting to recover real people, especially friends and colleagues, and that there are moral grey areas not sufficiently covered by phrases like "we do not negotiate with terrorists."

Brian Montopoli, "A Price to Pay for Negotiating with Terrorists?," CBS News. www.cbsnews.com.

Abu Sayyaf

Whereas the Chechens were focused on using hostage taking as a way to achieve a political outcome, separatists in the southern Philippines seemed more interested in kidnapping for money. There, a group called Abu Sayyaf made millions by ransoming hostages in the name of fighting for an independent Islamic state for the country's minority (5 to 9 percent)

Muslim population. Between March 2000 and June 2002, Abu Sayyaf took as many as two hundred people hostage throughout the Pacific region. This number included twenty-one foreigners at a diving resort on Sipadan Island, Malaysia, in April 2000 and three French journalists reporting on this situation in July 2000. (Though Malaysia and the Philippines are roughly 1,500 miles (2,414 km) across the sea from one another, raids on Malaysia by armed groups from the Philippines have long been common.) Abu Sayyaf released all of these hostages later the same year after being paid somewhere between $10 million and $25 million. (The exact amount and sources were never made public.)

The following year, on May 27, 2001, Abu Sayyaf kidnapped twenty people from the Dos Palmas beach resort on the Philippine island of Palawan, taking their captives by speedboat to a jungle hideout on another island, Basilan, before beginning to ransom them off. By November 2001, most of the Dos Palmas hostages had been set free in exchange for various payouts of cash. Among those still held were three Americans who had been vacationing at the resort, Guillermo Sobero and Martin and Gracia Burnham. The gunmen demanded $1 million in ransom money for their release, but Philippine and US authorities refused to pay. Eleven months after the kidnapping, however, the United States facilitated the payment of $300,000 in ransom from private sources. Nonetheless, the kidnappers did not release their hostages.

Rescue Efforts

Meanwhile, a rescue attempt by the Philippine military in August 2001 resulted in the deaths of several soldiers. Two months later the United States learned that the hostage takers had ties to the terrorist group al Qaeda, which had attacked America a month earlier, and Philippine authorities discovered the decapitated body of Guillermo Sobero in a shallow grave. Given the al Qaeda connections and the dangerous situation clearly faced by the remaining American hostages, the United States

Russian authorities methodically identify hundreds of children and adults killed in a school seizure and rescue effort in 2004. The Chechen separatists who took captive more than thirteen hundred people at the school sought an independent state.

decided to become involved in the crisis. In January 2002 several US military advisers and 660 American troops went to the Philippines to engage in training exercises with Philippine troops and to help plan an attack on Abu Sayyaf.

Philippine soldiers first struck the group's stronghold on the island of Basilan in May 2002. The kidnappers managed to escape with the Burnhams in tow, and for nine days they evaded the soldiers, first on Basilan and then on the island of Mindanao. But their food was running out, and the weather was against them. On the afternoon of June 7, 2002, the kidnappers struggled to erect tents in a pouring rain while the Burnhams—missionaries who had traveled to the Philippines to celebrate their eighteenth wedding anniversary—huddled together in a hammock. The couple had been hostages for 376 days, and they feared this day would be their last. Their captors had begun to talk about killing them.

Then a team of thirty-seven soldiers spotted the camp and began firing at Abu Sayyaf members, most of whom were killed. In the chaos Martin Burnham was shot in the chest and Gracia in the leg. Martin died in his wife's arms after the two of them slid down a hill trying to escape the gunfire. Gracia was subsequently rescued by the soldiers and airlifted out of the jungle by helicopter.

Money over Politics

Other parts of the world also saw militants turn to hostage taking as a way to make money. Beginning in 2006 in Nigeria, for example, various militant groups of the Niger delta kidnapped foreign oil workers and charged an average of $500,000 for every one released. But experts have noted that by the end of the decade, most hostage taking involved criminal rather than political motivations.

In 2010 Esme McAvoy and David Randall of the British newspaper the *Independent* reported that "the average hostage is more likely to be a Mexican seized by a drug cartel . . . or people like Paul and Rachel Chandler, the British couple from Tunbridge Wells [England] whose yacht was scooped up by Somalian pirates" than someone "taken to try to force the hand of their governments as part of some wider dispute, or to publicise the cause of an insurgency."[27] In part this was because hostage taking had shown itself to be so lucrative that it began to attract more criminals than militants to the activity. But it was also because hostage taking had proven itself to be largely unsuccessful in convincing governments to give in to terrorist demands.

Chapter THREE

Suicide Bombings

The 2000s marked a dangerous increase in suicide bombings, especially in Asia and the Middle East. In countries such as Israel, Iraq, and Afghanistan, shoppers, worshippers, and others felt the brunt of attacks by people who detonated explosives carried on their bodies or in backpacks. In 2007 alone—the deadliest year for suicide bombings according to the Combating Terrorism Center at West Point military academy—there were 535 such attacks. Between 2004 and 2008, when the largest number of suicide bombings in history occurred, thousands of civilians and hundreds of soldiers and police officers were killed or injured because of suicide bombings. Their killers might be men or women; sometimes even children were coerced or tricked into carrying and setting off explosives.

Most suicide bombers were recruited, trained, and equipped by an organization rather than acting on their own initiative. According to sociologist Michael Biggs, an expert in suicide bombings, "Since the early 1980s, suicide bombing has been taken up largely by Muslim insurgent and terrorist groups. The major exception was the Tamil Tigers, drawn from a Hindu population in Sri Lanka."[28] In early 2002 the Tamil Tigers (more formally known as the Liberation Tamil Tigers of Eelam) were responsible for roughly one-third of all suicide attacks in the world, as part of a fight to gain an independent state for Sri Lanka's Tamil ethnic group.

Most organizations that engage in suicide bombings profess political or religious motivations. The more immediate objective, however, is usually to cause the greatest possible amount of bloodshed, which in turn would "sow fear in civilian populations, thwart economic development, repulse non-governmental organizations, and provoke military retaliation," says Biggs. An attack that kills the carrier of the explosives has added benefits for the larger organization. As Biggs explains,

"Suicide attacks are . . . attractive for insurgent organizations because detonation removes the possibility that the perpetrator will be captured and interrogated."[29]

Not wanting evidence left behind that might lead to the organization's location or future plans is not the same as not wanting public credit for their actions. Such groups usually wanted their enemies to know who was behind the bombing. Consequently, many groups—particularly those connected to al Qaeda—publicly claimed responsibility for dozens of suicide bombings in the 2000s. Their claims were usually made on social networking sites or by issuing public statements to the media. In either case, suicide bombings often brought terrorist groups a great deal of publicity.

The USS *Cole*

One of the most publicized suicide bombings in history was the case of the USS *Cole*, a 500-foot-long (152 m), American guided-missile destroyer. On August 8, 2000, the ship left the United States for a five-month deployment in the Middle East. It passed through the Suez Canal and the Red Sea, then stopped to refuel in the port city of Aden, Yemen, on October 12. This required the ship to anchor offshore at a platform called a dolphin, which was run by a private company.

The ship moored at the dolphin at around 9:30 a.m., and an hour later it began taking on fuel—a process that would normally take four to five hours. But forty-seven minutes after refueling began, two men approached in a small inflatable boat similar to the ones used by harbor workers who might be helping with the refueling process. As they pulled up alongside the ship, the men stood and saluted the few sailors on deck. Then the raft blew up.

The explosion ripped a 40-foot by 60-foot (12 m by 18 m) hole in the side of the destroyer. Although the ship remained afloat, the two suicide bombers and seventeen sailors died from the blast. An additional thirty-nine crew members were injured. Experts now know that the small boat was carrying 400 to 700 pounds (181 to 318 kg) of explosives, probably molded along its hull, and the resulting blast caused $250 million in damages. Further studies revealed that C-4, an explosive not normally available to civilians, was used in the attack. To some experts, this suggested that the terrorist organization supporting the suicide bombers was sponsored by a government.

Investigation into the *Cole* attack revealed that the terrorists had unsuccessfully attempted to blow up another American destroyer, the USS *The Sullivans*, in January 2000. According to an informant to authorities in Yemen, the suicide bombers set out to meet that destroyer with the same plan in mind but had to turn back when their boat began taking on water. In this case, investigators said, the attackers were carrying so many explosives that the weight threatened to sink them.

Fears of a Second Attack

In the immediate aftermath of the *Cole* bombing, US authorities feared the possibility of another attack. The US Marines were ordered to the region to guard the disabled destroyer and the surviving sailors on board. Guards were also charged with protecting the US ambassador to Yemen, who was housed in a nearby hotel. Meanwhile, US politicians called for an investigation into the reasons that two unknown, unauthorized men were allowed to approach a US destroyer without being warned away or even shot at.

Under military rules of engagement at the time, US military personnel were not allowed to shoot at someone unless they were being shot at or had received specific orders in advance to shoot at such a target. Moreover, given anti-American sentiment in the region, there were political reasons for holding fire. Petty Officer Jennifer Kudrick, a sonar technician on the *Cole*, says, "We would have gotten in more trouble for shooting two foreigners than losing 17 American sailors."[30] After the *Cole* attack, the US military changed its rules of engagement and told soldiers and sailors to shoot at anyone perceived as a threat, even if that person was not shooting at them.

Claiming Responsibility

Three Islamic terrorist groups subsequently claimed responsibility for the *Cole* attack: the Aden-Abyan Islamic Army, the Army of Mohammed, and the Islamic Deterrence Forces. The Islamic Army was already well known for carrying out major operations; in 1998 the group kidnapped sixteen tourists in Yemen, four of whom died during a rescue attempt. However, the other two groups were previously unknown even to Yemeni

A gaping hole is visible in the hull of the USS Cole *after suicide bombers pulled up alongside the destroyer in a small, inflatable boat similar to the ones used by harbor workers and then detonated their explosives. The 2000 attack killed seventeen sailors and injured thirty-nine others.*

authorities. Some experts believe that the groups claiming responsibility were not actually responsible. Instead, these experts think al Qaeda was to blame for the bombings.

After the bombing, the leader of al Qaeda, Osama bin Laden, publicly praised the bombers and, at his son's wedding in January 2001, recited a poem about the attack:

A destroyer: even the brave fear its might.
It inspires horror in the harbour and in the open sea.
She sails into the waves
Flanked by arrogance, haughtiness and false power.
To her doom she moves slowly
A dinghy awaits her, riding the waves.[31]

Although there is no definitive proof that Bin Laden was behind the *Cole* attack, there is evidence that during the late 1990s he proposed attacking an American naval ship. Moreover, several men eventually arrested on suspicion of being involved in the *Cole* attack proved to have ties to al Qaeda, and US officials now say that the bombing was planned by Abd al-Rahim al-Nashiri, a high-level member of al Qaeda who was captured in Dubai, United Arab Emirates, in 2002.

The Tamil Tigers

Many terrorism experts believe that al Qaeda used the activities of the Tamil Tigers as a model for the *Cole* bombing. Using suicide bombers to attack ships was one of the Sri Lankan group's specialties, beginning with a 1990 attack on a naval vessel in Trincomalee, Sri Lanka. During the 1990s the Tamil Tigers pioneered the technique of fastening explosives to the bow of a boat, the approach that the *Cole* bombers later used, and in September 2001 the group employed approximately twenty such explosive-filled boats piloted by suicide bombers in an attack on the Sri Lankan navy. The Tigers also developed the idea of putting the explosives of suicide bombers into vests and belts, another technique subsequently adopted by Muslim terrorists.

In general, the actions of the Tamil Tigers received much less attention worldwide than other such attacks. That changed on November 28, 2007, when twenty-four-year-old Sujatha Vagawanam detonated a bomb in the office of Sri Lankan cabinet minister Douglas Devananda. Though Devananda, the target of the attack, was not in his office at the time, the bombing gained notoriety. Unbeknownst to Vagawanam, security cameras were recording the scene in the office when she blew herself up, making it the first fully videotaped suicide bombing.

Another Tigers suicide bombing that received widespread publicity occurred in Akuressa, near the Sri Lankan capital, on March 10, 2009. This, too, targeted government officials. On that day, several officials were at the Jumma Mosque participating in ceremonies honoring the birth of the prophet Muhammad. At around 10:30 that morning, the minister for posts and telecommunications, Mahinda Wijesekara; the former chief minister of the Southern Province (where Akuressa is located), H.G. Sirisena; and three other ministers were participating in a procession toward the mosque. As the group approached the building, a male suicide bomber detonated his explosives. The bomb, made of C-4 explosives, sprayed the crowd with tiny steel balls. Fourteen people were killed and forty-six others were injured. Among the injured were Wijesekara and Sirisena; the other ministers were unhurt.

The Assassination of Ahmad Shah Massoud

Several of the most notable suicide bombings in Afghanistan during the 2000s also targeted political leaders. According to a 2007 UN Assistance Mission in Afghanistan (UNAMA) report on suicide attacks in that country, the Afghan population first became aware of suicide bombing with the assassination of a prominent political and military leader, Ahmad Shah Massoud. The report states, "Before the assassination of Ahmad Shah Massoud on September 9th 2001, the notion that suicide might be used to kill others was considered alien. Indeed, when such attacks began appearing with regularity in 2005 and 2006, the community's initial response was to reject the possibility that Afghans themselves might be involved."[32]

Three weeks before the attack on Massoud—which took place just two days before al Qaeda's 9/11 attack on the United States—two men claiming to be reporters with an Arab news agency requested an interview with Massoud. At the time Massoud was the leader of the United Front, a group seeking to end Taliban rule in Afghanistan. The two had passports showing that their nationality was Moroccan and that they had traveled to Afghanistan by way of Belgium. In addition, members of Massoud's group had vouched for them. Therefore they were granted the interview, and while waiting for their appointment with Massoud, they interviewed two other prominent Afghan politicians, Burhanuddin Rabbani and Abdul Rasul Sayyaf.

Finally they sat down with Massoud at his base in northern Afghanistan, a video camera ready to record the interview. Journalist Sebastian Junger reported on what happened next:

Just before noon, with Massoud seated before them, they started the interview. Seconds later everyone in the room was either wounded or dead. The attackers had packed the camera with explosives and blown themselves up. Nothing remained of one but his legs; the other was killed as he fled. Massoud was horribly wounded but still alive. His men tried to rush him to a helicopter for the short flight to Tajikistan, but he survived only 15 minutes. . . . [He] passed from this life in the back of a battered Land Cruiser, racing through the mountains of Afghanistan.[33]

Another member of the United Front was killed in the blast as well.

Afterward an investigation revealed that the suicide bombers' passports had been stolen. They were probably Tunisian, but experts disagree on their identity. However, most believe that al Qaeda and/or the Taliban ordered the assassination. These experts theorize that the suicide bombers knew that 9/11 was about to happen and believed the United States would support Massoud's anti-Taliban efforts after the attack. With such support, Massoud would most likely have been able to overthrow the Taliban, thereby ending the regime's control of Afghanistan and its sponsorship of al Qaeda.

Carnage in Afghanistan

Suicide bombers associated with al Qaeda and the Taliban targeted several other political leaders in Afghanistan during the decade. Unlike the attack on Massoud, which killed two people, other suicide bombings resulted in many civilian deaths. In fact, the 2007 UNAMA report found that whereas most suicide bombings in Afghanistan were strikes against political and/or military targets, roughly 80 percent of the victims were civilians. This was the case with two of the most deadly suicide bombings of the decade.

The first occurred in November 2007 in the northern Afghan city of Baghlan, where local government officials, community elders, and schoolchildren had gathered to welcome a delegation of eighteen members of parliament at the opening of a sugar factory. As the group passed through a gate at the facility, a pair of suicide bombers detonated their explosives, killing at least seventy-five people and possibly more than ninety. Among the dead were sixty-two schoolchildren and all eight members of Parliament's National Economic Committee.

The blast also injured more than a hundred people, and many pregnant women who had been exposed to the blast subsequently miscarried or gave birth to infants with severe birth defects. This was because of the composition of the explosives. A surgeon who treated the victims later said, "The explosion was very strong, without any doubt chemical materials were used [to maximize the explosion]."[34] Other injured survivors lost limbs or eyesight and some struggled with depression, amnesia, and learning disabilities.

The target of the second major attack was Abdul Hakim Jan, an ex-police chief and anti-Taliban militia leader. On February 17, 2008, Jan decided to attend a dogfight in Kandahar, the second-largest city in Afghanistan and previously a Taliban stronghold. The Taliban had banned such fights, but after the regime's demise, they had become extremely popular, often attracting hundreds of spectators. On this day, a suicide bomber detonated his explosives in a large crowd of spectators, killing Jan and at least 80 other people and possibly as many as 105.

Iraq

The 2000s saw a massive rise in deaths and injuries caused by suicide bombings in Iraq—especially among that country's civilian population. According to a study by the *Lancet* in 2011, suicide bombings in Iraq killed sixty times more civilians than soldiers (at least twelve thousand as opposed to two hundred) from 2003 to 2010. Iraq also experienced a larger number of major suicide bombings than other countries. These bombings were carried out by extremist organizations—primarily al Qaeda, Ansar al-Sunna, and the Islamic State of Iraq—wanting to drive Westerners from the country. A majority of the bombings that killed a large number of people (over one hundred) occurred in the city of Baghdad.

Suicide Bombing Is a Social Ritual

The most common perception regarding suicide bombers is that they are mentally ill. However, as psychiatrist Noam Shpancer reports, "In most cases, evidence of what we would consider individual insanity or mental illness is not a feature of future suicide bombers' profiles." Instead, he argues, suicide bombers are a product of their society. "You are created in your society's image," he says. "Once society settles on a set of values and the accepted ways of obtaining them, individuals within the society, any society, are compelled to follow the path." He adds:

> [Suicide bombing] is not a crazed act of insane individuals, but a social ritual. While its proximal causes are shaped by the current parameters of a specific group, its ultimate causes emerge from the grouping impulse inherent in human nature. For a society (or a group) that perceives itself as engaged in a territorial or ideological struggle for its very survival against overpowering enemies, it is not irrational to embrace, promote and celebrate individual acts of great sacrifice for the cause; particularly if the enemy is deemed less than human, as all enemies are always deemed; particularly if those acts are intoxicatingly brutal; particularly if they are shown to be effective weapons in the fight. For individuals under the pressure of a society, and in the throes of true believerism, suicide bombing can become an attractive option."

Noam Shpancer, "Understanding the Suicide Bomber," *Psychology Today,* September 23, 2010. www.psychologytoday.com.

Many of Iraq's suicide bombings involved cars and trucks used as bombs. For example, on February 3, 2007, a man drove a food truck filled with explosives into a crowded outdoor marketplace. He timed his arrival to coincide with the last few minutes to buy food before an evening curfew, knowing this would cause people to rush his truck. Then he detonated it, killing himself and more than 130 civilians and wounding nearly 350 others.

by just a bit of flesh, hanging. I picked myself up to get help. I was bleeding heavily. I know that I needed someone to stop the bleeding. I caught my left hand with my right, but I slipped from all the mess on the floor.[39]

Suicide bombings surged in Israeli in the 2000s. Israeli police search the wreckage of a suicide bombing in Haifa. More than a dozen people died when a Palestinian suicide bomber detonated nail-studded explosives on the bus.

Eleven Israelis were killed in the blast. The force of the explosion was so great that workers wearing surgical gloves struggled the next day to find the remains of the dead in the gutted café. In addition, more than fifty people were injured in the bombing, and both they and people who lived in the area and/or had frequented the Moment Café were traumatized by the tragedy.

A week earlier another Palestinian suicide bomber had blown himself up in a crowd of mothers and babies in a devoutly Jewish neighborhood, killing nine. Shortly after that, a suicide bombing at a café in another neighborhood was thwarted after a waiter noticed that a man who was dressed in a heavy overcoat seemed nervous. The waiter shoved the man outside, tackled him, and ripped the bomb wires from the explosive device hidden under his coat. This incident received a great deal of publicity, calling attention to the need to be alert for potential suicide bombers, but it was not enough to prevent the deaths at the Moment Café.

Changing Attitudes

Suicide bombings occurred elsewhere throughout the decade. For example, in 2009 Pakistan experienced a series of marketplace attacks by suicide bombers. These were a response to Pakistani troop attacks that year on Taliban insurgents in the Waziristan region of the country as part of efforts to cooperate with the War on Terror.

On October 9 a suicide bomber in a car detonated his explosives at an outdoor market in Peshawar, killing 53 people. On October 28 another suicide car bomber killed 118 people at another Peshawar marketplace. A few days later a suicide bomber blew himself up at a cattle market in the village of Adazai, a suburb of Peshawar, killing the village's mayor and 17 others. Shortly after that a suicide car bomber killed 34 and injured at least 50 in a crowded market in Charsadda, northeast of Peshawar.

Perhaps as a result of these attacks, public opinion regarding suicide bombing changed. Pew Research polled people in seventeen countries in

2002 and 2009. In the 2002 poll a third of the respondents in Pakistan said that suicide bombing was justified in the defense of Islam. In 2009 nearly 90 percent said it was never justified. This was a major development in a country that had previously allowed terrorist organizations to establish bases within its borders.

Chapter FOUR

Coordinated Attacks

When people think of attacks from the 2000s, they most often recall those involving several targets hit at once as part of a carefully organized terrorist operation. This was the case, for example, with al Qaeda's 9/11 attack on America. Terrorists coordinated their efforts so that several planes were hijacked at once and then crashed into predetermined targets.

Coordinated terrorist attacks were almost nonexistent during the 1970s, but by the end of the 1990s they made up roughly 30 percent of all terrorist attacks. According to the National Consortium for the Study of Terrorism and Responses to Terrorism (START), this figure decreased to between 10 and 15 percent during the 2000s. At the same time, however, the coordinated attacks that occurred were more lethal than before. In fact, START reports that the coordinated attacks of the decade were 44 percent more lethal than uncoordinated ones.

In addition to 9/11, START names four coordinated terrorist attacks as being among the most lethal of the decade. These were the Bali nightclub bombings of 2002, the Madrid train bombings of 2004, the London transit attacks of 2005, and the Mumbai attacks of 2008. All but Mumbai were connected to al Qaeda.

The Bali Nightclub Bombings

On the night of October 12, 2002, dozens of people, most in their twenties or thirties, were partying in nightclubs in Kuta Beach, a tourist district on the Indonesian island of Bali. At around midnight, a man walked into Paddy's Irish Club and detonated a small explosive device that was hidden inside a backpack or a vest. The blast killed the bomber, injured the people around him, and caused the crowd to rush outside. Seconds later another suicide bomber detonated powerful explosives hidden inside a white Mitsubishi van parked in front of a neighboring nightclub, the Sari Club. Experts later determined that a third terrorist was watching the van from afar, holding a remote control device—possibly a doctored cell phone—that would allow him to detonate the van if the man inside of the vehicle lost his nerve.

The van bomb destroyed the Sari Club, blew a crater roughly 3 feet (1 m) deep into the street, and damaged surrounding buildings. Richard Poore, a New Zealander staying in a hotel more than 0.5 miles (.8 km) away, reported shortly after the blast, "The windows of the hotel blew out, the upper floors have lost their ceilings and dropped in, and there was an incredible amount of smoke in the sky." He and his wife, Giliana, rushed to help the victims at the nightclub, and later Poore said of the scene, "I have just never seen anything like it. It was horrendous. Total carnage."[40]

At least two hundred people suffered serious injuries, many of them severe burns from a fire that raged in and around both clubs. In addition, over two hundred people were killed, most of them foreign tourists. The majority of the dead were from Australia, but travelers from more than twenty other countries were killed as well.

There was an additional bombing in front of the American consulate building in nearby Denpasar, Bali's capital. A small explosive device left there was timed to go off in the moments between the other two bombs. One passerby was injured, but the bomb did little damage.

A subsequent investigation revealed that the bombers were members of a regional Islamic extremist group, Jemaah Islamiah (JI), believed to have close ties to al Qaeda. Over a dozen men were arrested as being part of the Bali plot; most were given jail sentences, but three were sentenced to death. This, however, did not prevent another JI-oordinated attack. On October 1, 2005, three suicide bombers from the group killed themselves and at least nineteen other people in Bali tourist areas.

The Madrid Train Bombings

The coordinated attack on trains in Madrid, Spain, on March 11, 2004, was a more elaborate operation than the Bali attack. The planners carried thirteen bombs, each hidden inside a backpack, onto four commuter

third unexploded bomb, also still within its backpack, was not found until much later, amidst some luggage that had been removed from a train car. All three bombs proved to be improvised explosive devices— a type of homemade bomb commonly used by terrorists—and experts used controlled detonations to destroy them.

PERSPECTIVES

Americans Have Given Up Too Much to Prevent Terrorist Attacks

After 9/11, the US government took various steps to prevent future terrorist attacks. For example, legal barriers were removed to make it easier to spy on individuals as well as to search, arrest, and detain them. Some people believe that these changes have threatened the very essence of American democracy. Jonathan Turley, a professor of public interest law at George Washington University, explains:

> In the decade since Sept. 11, 2001, this country has comprehensively reduced civil liberties in the name of an expanded security state. . . . At what point does the reduction of individual rights in our country change how we define ourselves?

> While each new national security power Washington has embraced was controversial when enacted, they are often discussed in isolation. But they don't operate in isolation. They form a mosaic of powers under which our country could be considered, at least in part, authoritarian. Americans often proclaim our nation as a symbol of freedom to the world while dismissing nations such as Cuba and China as categorically unfree. Yet, objectively, we may be only half right. Those countries do lack basic individual rights such as due process, placing them outside any reasonable definition of "free," but the United States now has much more in common with such regimes than anyone may like to admit.

Jonathan Turley, "Ten Reasons the U.S. Is No Longer the Land of the Free," *Washington Post*, January 15, 2012. http://articles.washingtonpost.com.

Americans Must Give Up Civil Liberties to Prevent Terrorist Attacks

In the months after 9/11, some Americans were unhappy that they had to give up civil liberties in order to prevent terrorism. Others, however, defended these sacrifices as the only way to ward off more attacks like 9/11. For example, in 2002 David Tucker, an associate professor of defense analysis at the Naval Postgraduate School and an adviser to the Ashbrook Center for Public Affairs, argued that although the War on Terror was designed to hunt down terrorists, if this effort was not successful in deterring future attacks "then we must increase our efforts to detect threats, reduce our vulnerability to them, minimize the danger they pose and increase our ability to recover from any attacks that might occur. . . . We cannot reduce this threat without reducing our freedom." He added that "increased power may help the government disrupt plots and make us more secure, even if it does not enable the government to disrupt all plots and make us perfectly secure."

Moreover, he suggested that the American public need not worry about the government going too far because its "homeland security strategy must do more than provide for the physical security of Americans. It must protect political, economic and individual liberties." Tucker concluded: "As long as we can vote the President out of office in a free and fair election, then we retain the minimum necessary to consider ourselves a free people."

David Tucker, "Freedom and Security in the Homeland," Ashbrook Center, October 2002. http://ashbrook.org.

Tracking Down Killers

Meanwhile, the Spanish media was speculating on who might have committed the attack. The common view among the general public was that the explosions were in retaliation for Spain's having recently stationed roughly fourteen hundred of its troops in Iraq as part of the War on Terror. Based on this belief, a majority voted in an election two days later to put a new antiwar government in power, and the country subsequently removed its troops from Iraq.

Government officials initially suspected that the blame for the attack rested with a group of Basque separatists—people of an ethnic group within Spain, the Basque, who want their ancestral land to be an independent country. But as more details surfaced, authorities concluded that a small group of Islamic extremists was responsible and that these extremists had been inspired by al Qaeda but were actually not associated with al Qaeda. By this time, however, al Qaeda was claiming responsibility for the attack.

On April 3, 2004, Spanish police raided an apartment in Leganés, south of Madrid, where they suspected the bombers might be staying. To avoid capture, the seven men inside set off bombs that killed not only themselves but also a Spanish special forces agent. The police eventually arrested others suspected of having been involved in the attack and put twenty-nine of them on trial. Seventeen were found guilty and three others were jailed for other terrorist activities. However, Spanish politicians and pundits began to suggest that the government had rushed to judgment in blaming Islamic terrorists for deaths that Basque separatists had actually caused, and controversy over who committed the bombings persisted for the rest of the decade. (In 2012 evidence surfaced that strongly suggested al Qaeda had approved the attack, devoted resources to it, and supervised its execution.)

London Transit Attacks

The attack on the London, England, transit system was similar to the one in Madrid, involving bombs on trains that were timed to go off during morning rush hour. On July 7, 2005, blasts occurred on three trains in three separate locations along the London Underground, the city's subway system. Nearly an hour after these simultaneous explosions, another explosion occurred, this one blowing up a double-decker bus near Tavistock Square, a public square in London's medical and academic quarter. This coordinated attack killed fifty-six people, including the bombers, and injured an additional seven hundred.

Among those who had experienced the carnage in the pitch-black underground was a man who gave his name only as Ian. He later told a reporter,

There were body parts everywhere. There were arms, there were legs, there were limbs and there was blood and there was huge amounts of screaming. If anyone thinks they've heard screaming before they've never heard that kind of screaming. This was the screaming of seriously injured dying people. It was an unnatural screaming sound. . . . You just couldn't see anything and there was just body on top of body and they were so heavy.[42]

Video Evidence

Footage from closed-circuit cameras around London subsequently showed that the attackers were four men between the ages of eighteen and thirty who drove rental cars to one train station, then boarded a train to the King's Cross station. (Police later found explosives in one of the rental cars.) Once the men reached their destination, they went their separate ways, each wearing an identical backpack, looking as though nothing were troubling them. "You would have thought they were going on a hiking holiday,"[43] a confidential source told a reporter with the *Guardian* newspaper after viewing the footage.

The man who ended up on the double-decker bus had apparently intended to take an underground train like his associates. But when he arrived at the station, the train was out of service, so he took the bus instead. From cell phone records, investigators learned that this bomber had tried to call the others before boarding the bus, but by then they had already detonated the explosives hidden in their backpacks.

Even though each man died in the blast, some of their personal identification survived, and this helped police determine who they were. All were British citizens, three of Pakistani descent and one born in Jamaica. Two were married with young children; the other two lived with close relatives. Three resided in or near Leeds, a city of over seven hundred thousand about 190 miles (306 km) north-northwest of London. One of the bombers, eighteen-year-old Hasib Mir Hussain, lived there with his brother and sister-in-law. When he did not come home from a trip to London with friends, his parents called a police emergency line to find out whether their son had been hurt in the attack. They were stunned to learn later that he had been one of the suicide bombers.

Two of the other bombers had made videotapes before the attack to explain their motives. Both tapes came to light when they were aired on the Arabic television network al-Jazeera, one in September 2005 and the other on the one-year anniversary of the attack. In the latter tape, which was apparently meant to air right after the attack, twenty-two-year-old bomber Shehzad Tanweer said, "What have you witnessed now is only the beginning of a string of attacks that will continue and become stronger . . . until you pull your forces out of Afghanistan and Iraq."[44]

Similarly, in the tape shown just two months after the attack, thirty-year-old bomber Mohammad Sidique Khan said:

> Your democratically elected governments continuously perpetrate atrocities against my people all over the world. And your support of them makes you directly responsible. . . . Until we feel security, you will be our targets. And until you stop the bombing, gassing, imprisonment and torture of my people we will not stop this fight. We are at war and I am a soldier. Now you too will taste the reality of this situation.[45]

Both tapes also featured a prominent al Qaeda member, Ayman al-Zawahiri, confirming that al Qaeda was involved in the attack, but experts disagreed on just what the extent of this involvement was.

The Mumbai Attack

The coordinated attack on India's commercial capital, Mumbai, unfolded quite differently from the attacks in Bali, Madrid, and London. Experts believe the attackers were members of Lashkar-e-Taiba, a large Islamic militant group operating out of Pakistan. The group's goal was to end India's control of Jammu and Kashmir, the northernmost state in India.

The multiday assault started on the evening of Wednesday, November 26, 2008. A few days earlier, ten young men from Pakistan, each armed with grenades, an AK-47 assault rifle, and an automatic revolver, had hijacked an Indian fishing trawler. The attackers had killed four crew

Chapter **FIVE**

Internal Conflict and Civil Strife

During the 2000s, the number of countries experiencing internal conflict, whereby factions within a country fought against one another, shrank even as the amount of violence within the afflicted countries grew. As the *Economist* reported shortly after the decade ended, "Although the world's population has expanded since 1990, numbers of interstate wars, civil wars and coups have fallen—as have the numbers of deaths in them. Fewer countries suffer large-scale violence, but the ones that do suffer repeatedly."[50]

Moreover, these countries that suffered repeatedly had often gone through similar conflicts in previous decades. In fact, according to civil strife expert James D. Fearon, of the thirty-nine countries that experienced a civil war during the decade, nearly all had also experienced civil war within the previous thirty years. In most cases, these wars were initiated by small rebel groups that did not need the support of the general public because, Fearson explains, "where states are less capable, rebel groups often appear to be able to operate without broad or deep social support, or they can coerce it."[51]

The capability of a state to combat rebels is often dependent on whether it has the resources necessary to support its military and police forces. Consequently, while the reasons internal conflicts begin and continue are complex, they most often occur in poor counties. Some experts believe that when coupled with unemployment, poverty can also make it more likely for young men to form or join rebel groups.

Other experts have noted that just as poverty can cause civil strife, so too can civil strife cause poverty. For example, the Global Poverty Project, an action group fighting extreme poverty throughout the world, has noted that violent conflict "destroys societies and is a shortcut to extreme poverty. The destruction and chaos that violent conflict brings leads to lawlessness and human rights atrocities and the erosion, diversion or destruction of resources—natural, human, financial or infrastructure—limits people's access to basic needs, such as health, education and food."[52]

Colombia

In the South American nation of Colombia, poverty and other forces contributed to a decades-old conflict that involved three factions: left-wing guerrillas, right-wing paramilitary groups, and government military forces. The guerrillas belonged to a group called the Revolutionary Armed Forces of Colombia (FARC), which had been formed by peasants during the 1960s after soldiers began attacking rural villages supportive of communism. As FARC battled the military, it took control of more and more parts of the country, and wealthy landowners decided that the guerrillas were a threat to their property. Consequently, they created and funded paramilitary groups charged with killing as many guerrillas as possible.

The landowners typically paid paramilitary commanders for every dead FARC member presented to them, and the government sometimes rewarded its soldiers with promotions or holidays for the same practice. Often this led to abuses. In October 2008, for example, fake recruiters for a nonexistent work detail duped eleven young men from poor families into leaving their homes in a suburb of Bogotá. Their corpses were later found in a shallow grave, dressed in FARC uniforms. No one ever learned who killed them, but the people responsible were probably rewarded by members of either the government or the paramilitary.

Even women and children sometimes suffered this fate. In June 2007 soldiers attacked the house of Maria Ortega and killed her. Shortly thereafter her adult daughter, Claudia Ortega, went to the house expecting to see her mother's body, but she discovered it had already been identified as the body of a guerrilla and taken away. "My mother had nothing to do with the guerrillas," Ortega later said. "They said she gave medical support to them, but she was a farmer. She didn't even know how to give an injection."[53]

Left-wing FARC rebels march through a guerrilla camp deep in the Colombian jungle in 2001. A long-running war between the rebels and government-sponsored paramilitary groups brought renewed violence to Colombia in the 2000s.

Claudia Ortega's husband, Elias, said that of the twelve other guerrillas the army claimed were killed that day, "only four of those men were guerrillas. The rest were local boys who were cleaning the channels by the side of the road. But by the time the families got to the graveyard, they were already buried." Elias complained about the callousness of the killers. "They don't care about us as people," he said. "They just want to say, 'We killed 20, 30 guerrillas,' and get the promotions. If what they say was true, there'd be no guerrillas left and the war would be over."[54]

FARC responded to such actions by becoming increasingly violent. According to a 2009 study by New Rainbow, a Bogotá policy group, the number of ambushes, killings, plantings of land mines, and other guerrilla activities performed by the group increased from twelve hundred in 2008 to sixteen hundred in 2009. The group also attempted to assassinate several South American officials, and in December 2009 it succeeded in killing the governor of Caquetá, a Colombian state. He was shot by guerrillas who had stormed into his home dressed in jungle camouflage and carrying assault rifles. In addition, FARC continued to engage in its long-held practice of kidnapping high-profile civilians and holding them under deplorable conditions—often in jungle cages—until someone paid for their release. Among its most prominent captives was presidential candidate Ingrid Betancourt, who was taken in February 2002 and finally rescued by Colombian security forces in July 2008.

Darfur

According to a 2009 UN Refugee Agency report, by the end of 2008, 26 million people had been displaced by violent conflicts within their own countries. Among these were the inhabitants of Darfur, a region of North Africa's western Sudan. This region has been populated for centuries by dozens of indigenous ethnic groups and Arab migrants who coexisted and, in some cases, even intermarried. But conflicts over resources and livestock developed between indigenous and Arab populations who were suffering from thirty years of drought. Rebel groups formed to demand that the Sudanese government help and protect Darfur's indigenous peoples. Feeling threatened by the rebel groups, the government mobilized a largely Arab militia called the Janjaweed, according to the UN High Commissioner for Human Rights. The Janjaweed's purpose was to target and attack civilian populations represented by the rebel groups.

Beginning in 2003 and lasting much of the decade, the non-Arab indigenous peoples of Darfur were subjected to vicious attacks by the Janjaweed. Militia members brutally raped, tortured, and killed thousands of people and cut off food supplies to their towns so that anyone left alive would starve to death. In some cases, soldiers even dragged survivors of the violence out of hospitals in order to brutalize them

the gathering dressed in a combat uniform and carrying an M-16 assault rifle and other weapons. He then began shooting people.

Dipendra's first target was the king; the prince shot his father three times. A witness to the massacre, Rajiv Raj Shahi—the son-in-law of the king's youngest brother—later said, "I rushed to His Majesty, took off my coat and pressed it against his neck from where he was bleeding. He told me he had been shot in the stomach as well, probably the last words he spoke."[58]

The prince killed nine people during the shooting spree, which lasted roughly a minute and a half, and wounded three others. His victims were all members of the royal family and included his mother, brother, and sister. After killing his mother and brother, who confronted him outside as he was trying to leave the scene, Dipendra went to a small bridge that

PERSPECTIVES

Reducing Poverty Will Not End Civil Wars

Whereas some people believe that humanitarian efforts are the way to end civil wars, others disagree. For example, after studying the issue, Simeon Djankov, an economist with the World Bank, and Marta Reynal-Querol, an associate professor of economics and business at the Universitat Pompeu Fabra in Barcelona, Spain, reported in 2008 that previous research suggesting a correlation between poverty and civil war was flawed. They concluded that the results of their own studies "indicate that policies that are directed to increase per capita income will not have any effect in reducing the probability of civil war." The two added that "even if poverty were the main determinant of conflict, it would be very difficult to act on this determinant. Instead, policies need to address structural problems that make countries more prone to conflict." These structural problems, they said, were primarily those that exacerbated ethnic differences, such as institutions that favor one ethnic group over another and/or settlement patterns that put one ethnic group in direct competition with another for resources.

Simeon Djankov and Marta Reynal-Querol, "Poverty and Civil Wars," Vox, October 28, 2008. www.voxeu.org.

spanned a stream on the palace grounds and shot himself. He died three days later, whereupon his uncle Gyanendra became king.

A Deposed King

Whereas the former king had agreed to rule in concert with a royal parliamentary government, the new king chafed under this system. As a result, he had difficulty working with his government and kept dismissing prime ministers. In February 2005 King Gyanendra dismissed his parliament altogether, declared martial law, and made himself absolute ruler of the country.

In response, people blockaded roads and engaged in public protests. When these protests did nothing to change the political situation, Communist rebels called for a nationwide strike and many Nepalese obliged. The strike lasted two days, during which the king imposed a curfew and decreed that anyone caught outside between the hours of 10 p.m. and 9 a.m. would be shot on sight. This caused only more outrage and resistance among the populace. In April 2006 the king realized he was losing control of his country and reinstated the parliament. Two years later, on May 29, 2008, his government voted to depose him and made Nepal a parliamentary republic.

Thailand

The Southeast Asian nation of Thailand began the new decade with a house and senate made up of directly elected members for the first time in its history. In January 2001 the Thai Rak Thai political party, led by Thaksin Shinawatra, received the most votes in a national election, and Thaksin therefore became prime minister. He was elected to a second term in January 2005.

Shortly after his reelection, however, Thaksin's political enemies accused him of corruption and nepotism (favoring family members by way of political decisions and appointments). They also accused him of violating a law that required political candidates to disclose all of their assets prior to an election. With this accusation, Thaksin's enemies sought to invalidate his reelection. Thaksin, though, insisted that the lack of disclosure had resulted from a simple clerical error.

The judges charged with deciding his case allowed him to take office for his second term.

But this did not end the accusations and criticisms. When Thaksin sued a newspaper for printing a monk's sermon that suggested he was trying to take over the country, people accused the prime minister of censorship. When he performed an official ceremony that many people felt should have been performed by the king, people said he wanted to get rid of the king. When he claimed emergency powers in order to crush an ethnic separatist insurgency in southern Thailand, he was accused of abusing his power. Such sentiments led to anti-Thaksin demonstrations and protests, many of which were attended by several thousand people, as well as calls for Thaksin's resignation and attempts to impeach him.

Military Ousts Prime Minister

In August 2006 there were also unsuccessful attempts to kill Thaksin using car bombs. In one case, an explosives-filled car had been parked under a raised road on a route that the prime minister's motorcade was scheduled to travel, and the bomb was rigged to be detonated by remote control. However, it was discovered before the prime minister was in the area, and the car was later found to belong to an army officer. In another case, a man was caught driving a bomb-laden car near Thaksin's house and the bomb was defused. The would-be bomber was later found to be the chauffeur of a military general.

In September 2006, the military seized control of the government while the prime minister was attending a UN meeting in New York. The coup began when fifty soldiers of the Royal Thai Army stormed the building in Bangkok that houses the offices of the prime minister and his cabinet ministers. Once inside, the soldiers forced approximately 250 policemen to surrender their weapons. The military took over other parts of the city as well and arrested the deputy prime minister and the defense minister.

Thaksin did not return home but went into exile in Britain. Meanwhile, Thailand remained in turmoil. The military junta (members of the military who rule a country after seizing the government) reestablished a constitutional government but retained the power to get rid of any prime minister at will, and the country remained under martial law until January 2007. In December 2007 a democratic election was allowed, but a court later found that the winning political party was guilty of election fraud. That party was then dissolved, whereupon another political party took control and formed a new government. The decade ended with violent protests against this government as well as bomb attacks on government buildings.

Haiti

Experts say that violent public protests are far more likely in countries where governments are unstable. For example, according to the *Economist,* "Protests during the 2007–08 food-price crisis were more frequent and more likely to turn violent in countries with the most fragile governments."[59] This global crisis occurred when world food prices increased dramatically, and one of the places where the rising prices caused violent civil unrest was Haiti.

This island nation in the Caribbean has a population of over 9 million people, many of whom live in poverty. Haiti experienced roughly 50 percent increases in the cost of rice, beans, fruit, and other items in late 2007. By April 2008 Haitians' frustrations with this situation triggered violent riots. In one riot, protesters broke windows, looted shops, and burned cars. In another they tried to break into the presidential palace in the capital city of Port au Prince, demanding that President René Préval step down. UN peacekeepers fired rubber bullets into the crowd and used tear gas in efforts to quell the violence. Afterwards Préval remained in office, but the Haitian Senate subsequently dismissed his prime minister for failing to deal adequately with the crisis.

Such political turmoil was not new for Haiti. Earlier in the decade, in 2004, President Jean-Bertrand Aristide was forced out of office shortly after a majority of the population had reelected him. His ouster was orchestrated by wealthy Haitians who disapproved of Aristide's efforts to help the poor and raise their pay. Aristide told his supporters, most of whom were poor and dark skinned, "You are peasants; you are poor. You are the same color I am. They [upper-class Haitians] don't like you. . . . Your children are not children of big shots. They don't like you."[60]

However, Aristide also believed that the opposition against him was partly due to Haiti's habit of not letting anyone stay in power very long. In December 2002 he told the *New York Times*, "We still have some consequences from that past where we had 32 coups d'état. It is not easy for all the political parties to forget about that bad way to behave, moving from one coup d'état to another."[61]

In fact, another coup did occur, after Aristide opponents engaged in armed attacks that made it appear as though his government was about to fall. As rebels took control of entire cities, Aristide left Haiti. Early reports said that he fled of his own accord, but Aristide later said that US troops forced him to leave after telling him it was the only way to end the bloodshed. In either case, after Aristide left, a military junta took control of the country, and efforts to help the poor ended.

Humanitarian Aid

During the 2000s outsiders stepped in to provide aid to some of those suffering from civil strife. In fact, more money was spent on humanitarian aid in that decade than ever before. According to Joshua S. Goldstein of *Foreign Policy* magazine, "The humanitarian dollars spent per displaced person rose in real terms from $150 in the early 1990s to $300 in 2006. Total international humanitarian assistance has grown from $2 billion in 1990 to $6 billion in 2000 and (according to donor countries' claims) $18 billion in 2008. For those caught in the crossfire, war has actually gotten more humane."[62] However, no amount of money or compassion could bring back a loved one killed in a civil war or a violent act of civil unrest, nor could it reduce the number of victims of internal conflicts.

Source Notes

Introduction: A Climate of Fear

1. Quoted in John Mueller, "A False Sense of Insecurity?," *Regulation*, Fall 2004, pp. 42–46. http://politicalscience.osu.edu.

2. Quoted in Michael Collett and Matthew Liddy, "9/11 Eyewitness Shares Never-Seen-Before Photos," Australian Broadcasting Commission News, September 9, 2011. www.abc.net.au.

3. Quoted in Collett and Liddy, "9/11 Eyewitness Shares Never-Seen-Before Photos."

4. Quoted in Michael Ellison, Ed Vulliamy, and Jane Martinson, "'We Got Down to the Outside and It Was Like an Apocalypse,'" *Guardian* (Manchester, UK), September 12, 2001. www.guardian.co.uk.

5. Ellison, Vulliamy, and Martinson, "'We Got Down to the Outside and It Was Like an Apocalypse.'"

6. Scott Atran, "Enemies," *The Chronicle Review*, August 7, 2011, http://chronicle.com/article/Era-in-Ideas-Enemies/128499.

Chapter One: The War on Terror

7. Quoted in 9/11 Memorial Website, "Quotes 1." www.911-remember.com.

8. Quoted in Mark Halperin, "Transcript: CNN National Security Debate," The Page, *Time*, November 23, 2011. http://thepage.time.com.

9. Quoted in About.com, "Full Text; President Bush Declares 'War on Terror'; Speech to a Joint Session of Congress, Sept. 20, 2001. http://middleeast.about.com.

10. Quoted in Associated Press, "Afghanistan's Female Bombing Victims," October 15, 2001. http://archives.econ.utah.edu.

11. Quoted in Associated Press, "Afghanistan's Female Bombing Victims."

12. Quoted in Robert Collier, "Baghdad Closer to Collapse," *San Francisco Chronicle*, April 9, 2003. www.sfgate.com.

13. Collier, "Baghdad Closer to Collapse."

14. Quoted in BBC News, "How Saddam Hussein Was Captured," December 15, 2003. http://news.bbc.co.uk.

15. Quoted in Office of the Press Secretary, "President Bush Releases National Strategy for Combating Terrorism," press release, February 14, 2003. http://georgewbush-whitehouse.archives.gov.

16. Brown University, "'Costs of War' Project: Estimated Cost of Post-9/11 Wars; 225,000 Lives, up to $4 Trillion," press release, June 29, 2011. http://news.brown.edu.

17. Carol Rosenberg, "Guantánamo: The Most Expensive Prison on Earth," *Miami Herald*, November 25, 2011. www.miamiherald.com.

18. Quoted in Reza Sayah, "Iran Winning from War on Terror, Analysts Say," CNN, September 13, 2011. www.cnn.com.

Chapter Two: Hostage Taking

19. Minwoo Yun, "Hostage Taking and Kidnapping in Terrorism: Predicting the Fate of a Hostage," *Professional Issues in Criminal Justice,* 2007. https://kucampus.kaplan.edu/documentstore/docs09/pdf/picj/vol2/issue1/Hostage_Taking_and_Kidnapping_in_Terrorism.pdf.

20. Julie Rawe et al. "Iraq: The Sad Tale of Nick Berg," *Time,* May 24, 2004. www.time.com.

21. Quoted in Tides World Press, "Video of American Nick Berg's Executioner's Statement," Why War?, May 11, 2004. www.why-war.com.

22. Quoted in Mail Foreign Service, "British Hostage Released ALIVE After 'Unspeakable' Two-and-a-Half Years," *Mail Online,* December 30, 2009. www.dailymail.co.uk

23. Rebecca Leung, "Terror in Moscow," *60 Minutes,* CBS News, February 11, 2009. www.cbsnews.com.

24. Quoted in *LiveLeak* [blog], "Eight Years Ago: Chechens Take Hostages in Moscow Theater Part I," November 3, 2010. www.liveleak .com.

25. Quoted in Leung, "Terror in Moscow."

26. *Guardian* [Manchester, UK], "Timeline: The Beslan School Siege," September 6, 2004. www.guardian.co.uk.

27. Esme McAvoy and David Randall, "The £1 Billion Hostage Trade," *Independent* (London), October 17, 2010. www.independent.co.uk.

Chapter Three: Suicide Bombings

28. Michael Biggs, "Ultimate Sacrifice," *Foreign Policy,* December 16, 2012. www.foreignpolicy.com.

29. Biggs, "Ultimate Sacrifice."

30. Quoted in Stephen Robinson, "Bombed US Warship Was Defended by Unloaded Guns," *Telegraph* (UK), November 15, 2000. www.telegraph .co.uk.

31. Quoted in Brian Whitaker, "Attack on the USS *Cole*: The Bin Laden Connection," al-Bab. www.al-bab.com.

32. UN Assistance Mission in Afghanistan, "Suicide Attacks in Afghanistan (2001–2007)," September 9, 2007. www.unhcr.org.

33. Sebastian Junger, "Sebastian Junger on Afghanistan's Slain Rebel Leader," *National Geographic*, March/April 2001. www.nationalgeo graphic.com.

34. Quoted in Hadi Kazimi, "Baghlan Residents Still Suffering Three Years After 2007 Suicide Attack," RAWA News, March 22, 2011. www.rawa.org.

35. Carolyn E. Price, "Truck Bomb Kills More than 120 in Baghdad Market," Digital Journal, February 3, 2007. http://m.digitaljournal .com.

36. Quoted in Price, "Truck Bomb Kills More than 120 in Baghdad Market."

37. Joe Stork, "Erased in a Moment: Suicide Bombing Attacks Against Israeli Civilians," Human Rights Watch, 2002. www.hrw.org.

38. Quoted in BBC News, "Suicide Attack Hits Jerusalem Café," March 10, 2002. http://news.bbc.co.uk.

39. Quoted in Stork, "Erased in a Moment."

Chapter Four: Coordinated Attacks

40. Quoted in BBC News, "Dozens Killed in Bali Nightclub Explosion," October 12, 2002. http://news.bbc.co.uk.

41. Quoted in BBC News, "Scores Die in Madrid Bomb Carnage," March 11, 2004. http://news.bbc.co.uk.

42. Quoted in BBC News, "Reliving the London Bombing Horror," October 16, 2005. http://news.bbc.co.uk.

43. Duncan Campbell and Sandra Laville, "British Suicide Bombers Carried Out London Attacks, Say Police," *Guardian* (Manchester, UK), July 12, 2005. www.guardian.co.uk.

44. Quoted in *Guardian* (Manchester, UK), "Video of London Bomber Released," July 6, 2006. www.guardian.co.uk.

45. Quoted in BBC News, "London Bomber: Text in Full," September 1, 2005. http://news.bbc.co.uk.

46. Quoted in BBC News, "Eyewitness: Mumbai Survivors," November 29, 2008. http://news.bbc.co.uk.

47. Quoted in BBC News, "Mumbai Attacks: One Year on," November 29, 2009. http://news.bbc.co.uk.

48. Quoted in Somini Sengupta, "Dossier Gives Details of Mumbai Attacks," *New York Times,* January 6, 2009. www.nytimes.com.

49. Quoted in BBC News, "As It Happened: Mumbai Attacks 27 November 27, 2008." http://news.bbc.co.uk.

Chapter Five: Internal Conflict and Civil Strife

50. *Economist,* "The Economics of Violence," April 14, 2011. www.econ omist.com.

51. James D. Fearon, "Governance and Civil War Onset," World Bank, August 31, 2010. http://siteresources.worldbank.org.

52. Global Poverty Project, "Conflict and Poverty." www.globalpoverty project.com.

53. Quoted in Mike Power, "The Devastation of Colombia's Civil War," *Guardian* (Manchester, UK), April 22, 2011. www.guardian.co.uk.

54. Quoted in Power, "The Devastation of Colombia's Civil War."

55. Quoted in *Times Colonist* (Victoria, B.C.), "Survivor of Darfur Horror Rejects Calls for Her Silence," September 21, 2008. www.canada.com.

56. Quoted in Wire Services, "Congo Beats Back Coup," *St. Petersburg (FL) Times,* June 12, 2004. www.sptimes.com.

57. Quoted in Jo Adetunji, "Fierce Fighting Spreads Across East Congo," *Guardian* (Manchester, UK), November 6, 2008, www.guardian.co.uk.

58. Quoted in Damakant Jayshi, "Eyewitness Confirms Dipendra as Killer," *Gulf News* (Dubai, UAE), June 8, 2001. http://gulfnews.com.

59. *Economist,* "The Economics of Violence," April 14, 2011. www.econ omist.com.

60. GlobalSecurity.org, "Jean-Bertrand Aristide (2000–2004)," www .globalsecurity.org.

61. GlobalSecurity.org, "Jean-Bertrand Aristide (2000–2004)," www .globalsecurity.org.

62. Joshua S. Goldstein, "Think Again: War," *Foreign Policy,* September /October 2011. www.foreignpolicy.com.

Important People: Terrorism and War of the 2000s

Osama bin Laden: As leader of the terrorist group al Qaeda, he masterminded the 9/11 attacks on the World Trade Center and the Pentagon and was behind several other terrorist bombings during the 2000s. He was killed by US Navy SEALs on May 2, 2011.

Anthony Charles Lynton "Tony" Blair: British prime minister from 1997 to 2007, he was a major supporter of the foreign policies of US president George W. Bush and contributed British troops to both the 2001 invasion of Afghanistan and the 2003 invasion of Iraq.

George W. Bush: President of the United States from 2001 through 2008, he was instrumental in launching the War on Terror after 9/11. He also signed the Patriot Act into law in October 2001, thereby giving law enforcement and intelligence agencies more power to combat terrorism.

Richard Bruce "Dick" Cheney: As vice president of the United States from 2001 through 2008, he played a key role in developing the US response to 9/11 and helped orchestrate the War on Terror. After leaving office he became a vocal defender of his administration's antiterrorism efforts.

Gyanendra Bir Bikram Shah Dev: After the massacre of much of Nepal's royal family in 2001, he became king of Nepal but ruled in concert with a parliament under a constitutional monarchy. In 2005, however, he dismissed his parliament and tried to become absolute ruler of his country. After much political turmoil, he was deposed in 2008.

Saddam Hussein: President and dictator of Iraq from July 1979 to April 2003, he was accused of developing weapons of mass destruction and of having ties to the terrorist group al Qaeda. Neither of these accusations was ever proven to be true. Nonetheless, in March 2003 a coalition of

US- and UK-led forces invaded Iraq and Saddam fled. He was captured in December 2003 and executed in Iraq in 2006.

Abd al-Rahim al-Nashiri: A high-level operative in the terrorist group al Qaeda, he is believed to have masterminded the attack on the USS *Cole* in 2000. He was captured in 2002 in the city of Dubai in the United Arab Emirates and is being held in the US military's Guantánamo Bay detention camp.

Barack Obama: Upon his inauguration as president of the United States in January 2009, he became responsible for managing conflicts that arose from the War on Terror, including the wars in Afghanistan and Iraq, and in December 2011 he succeeded in ending the Iraq War.

Mullah Mohammed Omar: The spiritual leader of the Taliban—a fundamentalist Muslim movement that controlled Afghanistan—this Muslim clergyman (*mullah*) was head of the country until late 2001, when he fled after being accused of sheltering terrorist Osama bin Laden. He then became the leader of insurgents attacking US forces in Afghanistan. In 2011 unnamed informants claimed Omar was no longer alive, but US officials could not confirm this report.

Vladimir Putin: As president of Russia from 2000 to 2008, he faced two major hostage crises, one in a Moscow theater in 2002 and the other at a Beslan school in 2004. Putin was criticized for his handling of these crises because many of the hostages died as a result of inept rescue operations. However, he was also lauded for increasing antiterrorism efforts against the Chechen separatists responsible for these events.

Donald Rumsfeld: Secretary of defense from 2001 to 2006, he made many important military decisions in the aftermath of 9/11 and oversaw the actions of US troops fighting wars in Afghanistan, Iraq, and elsewhere. He was also responsible for making decisions regarding the detention and interrogation of military prisoners, including those housed at Guantánamo Bay.

Abu Musa'b al-Zarqawi: An Islamic terrorist from Jordan, he masterminded terrorist attacks, suicide bombings, kidnappings, and beheadings in Iraq during the first half of the decade. Among the most publicized of his activities was the kidnapping of American Nick Berg in Iraq in 2004. In June 2006 al-Zarqawi was killed when a US Air Force jet dropped bombs on a safe house where he was meeting with associates.

Ayman al-Zawahiri: A close associate of Osama bin Laden, he is believed to have played a role in the 9/11 attacks and many other al Qaeda operations, including the 2005 coordinated attack on the London transit system. In 2011, after Bin Laden's death, Islamic websites reported that al-Zawahiri had been made the head of al Qaeda, a position he apparently continues to hold.

Words of the 2000s

Note: Below is a sampling of new words or words given new meaning during the decade, taken from a variety of sources.

bailout: Rescue by government of companies on the brink of failure.

birther: A person who believes that Barack Obama was not born in the United States and therefore cannot be president.

bling: Ostentatious displays of fortune and flash.

blog: A weblog.

chad: The tiny paper square that pops out when a voter punches the ballot card while casting a vote.

Chinglish: The growing Chinese-English hybrid language resulting from China's expanding influence.

click-through: Clicking on a banner ad on a website.

cloud computing: The practice of storing regularly used computer data on multiple servers that can be accessed through the Internet.

distracted driving: Multitasking while driving.

frenemy: Someone who is both friend and enemy.

generica: Strip malls, motel chains, prefab housing, and other features of the American landscape that are the same nationwide.

hacktivism: Activism by hackers.

hashtag: The # (hash) symbol used as a tag on Twitter.

helicopter mom/dad: A parent who micromanages his or her children's lives and is perceived to be hovering over every stage of their development.

locavore: Someone who cooks and eats locally grown food.

meh: Boring, apathetic, or unimpressive.

plutoed: To be demoted or devalued, as happened to the former planet Pluto.

push present: An expensive gift given to a woman by her husband in appreciation for having recently given birth.

red state/blue state: States whose residents predominantly vote Republican (red states) or Democrat (blue states).

same-sex marriage: Marriage of gay couples.

sandwich generation: People in their forties or fifties who are caring for young children and elderly parents at the same time.

sexting: Sending of sexually explicit text messages and pictures via cell phones.

snollygoster: A shrewd, unprincipled person; often used to refer to a politician.

staycation: A holiday spent at home and involving day trips to local attractions.

truthiness: Something one wishes to be the truth regardless of the facts.

tweet: To send a message via Twitter.

twixters: Adult men and women who still live with their parents.

unfriend: To remove someone from a friends list on a social networking site such as Facebook.

zombie bank: A financial institution kept alive only through government funding.

For Further Research

Books

Daron Acemoglu and James A. Robinson, *Why Nations Fail.* New York: Crown, 2012.

Damon DiMarco, *Tower Stories: An Oral History of 9/11.* Santa Monica, CA: Santa Monica, 2007.

William E. Dyson, *Terrorism: An Investigator's Handbook.* 4th ed. Waltham, MA: Anderson, 2011.

Jeffrey William Lewis, *The Business of Martyrdom: A History of Suicide Bombing.* Annapolis, MD: Naval Institute, 2012.

John Dramani Mahama, *My First Coup d'État: And Other True Stories from the Lost Decades of Africa.* New York: Bloomsbury, 2012.

Gus Martin, *Understanding Terrorism.* Thousand Oaks, CA: Sage, 2012.

Patricia D. Netzley, *The Greenhaven Encyclopedia of Terrorism.* San Diego, CA: Greenhaven Press, 2007.

Websites

BBC News, "London Attacks" (http://news.bbc.co.uk/2/hi/in_depth/uk/2005/london_explosions/default.stm). This site provides links to a variety of stories about the London transit attacks.

BBC News, "Mumbai Attacks" (http://news.bbc.co.uk/2/hi/in_depth/south_asia/2008/mumbai_attacks/default.stm). This BBC News website provides links to a variety of stories about the Mumbai attacks.

FBI, "Terrorism" (www.fbi.gov/about-us/investigate/terrorism). This website offers information on how the FBI fights terrorism.

Naval History & Heritage Command (www.history.navy.mil/special %20highlights/usscole/cole-index.htm). This naval history website provides complete information on the USS *Cole*, including details about its terrorist attack.

9/11 Memorial Website (www.911-remember.com). This website provides information and quotes related to the 9/11 terrorist attack and its victims.

Index

Note: Boldface page numbers indicate illustrations.

Picture Credits

About the Author

Patricia D. Netzley is the author of over fifty books for teens and adults. She also teaches writing and is a member of the Society of Children's Book Writers.